THIS BOOK BELONGS TO

3 COLORS SERIES. TRAVEL.
Stress-free color by number book, 3x3 mm. sections.

Meet the 3d stress-free color by number book from the 3 COLORS Series, where **you need to use just 3 colors.**

In this particular book, there are 25 amazing sightseeing from all over the world! **Don't limit yourself, just create!**

You should follow the simple rule, where:

#1 is a Light color

#2 is some Middle color

#3 is a Dark color.

For example:

You can choose 3 colors from the red shades pallet set, where №1 light is pink, №2 middle is scarlet, №3 dark is dark red. For your convenience, the 7 most widespread variants of pallet sets are placed on the back cover.

OR you can create your own 3 colors pallet set following the rule above.

Choose the most comfortable way of coloring: the typical way block coloring, the X-method, the DOTS method, or mixed. It is very relaxing and with fantastic very detailed results.

HAPPY COLORING!

TRY YOUR PALETTE

Choose one of these sets or create yours, following the simple rule:
#1 – Light
#2 – Middle
#3 – Dark

#1 – Light	#2 – Middle	#3 – Dark
1 Gray	2 Dark Gray	3 Black
1 Lilac	2 Violet	3 Purple
1 Pink	2 Scarlet	3 Dark Red
1 Flaxen	2 Yellow	3 Dark Yellow
1 Peach	2 Skin Tone	3 Brown
1 Light Blue	2 Blue	3 Dark Blue
1 Light Green	2 Green	3 Dark Green

CONTENT

The Statue
of Liberty

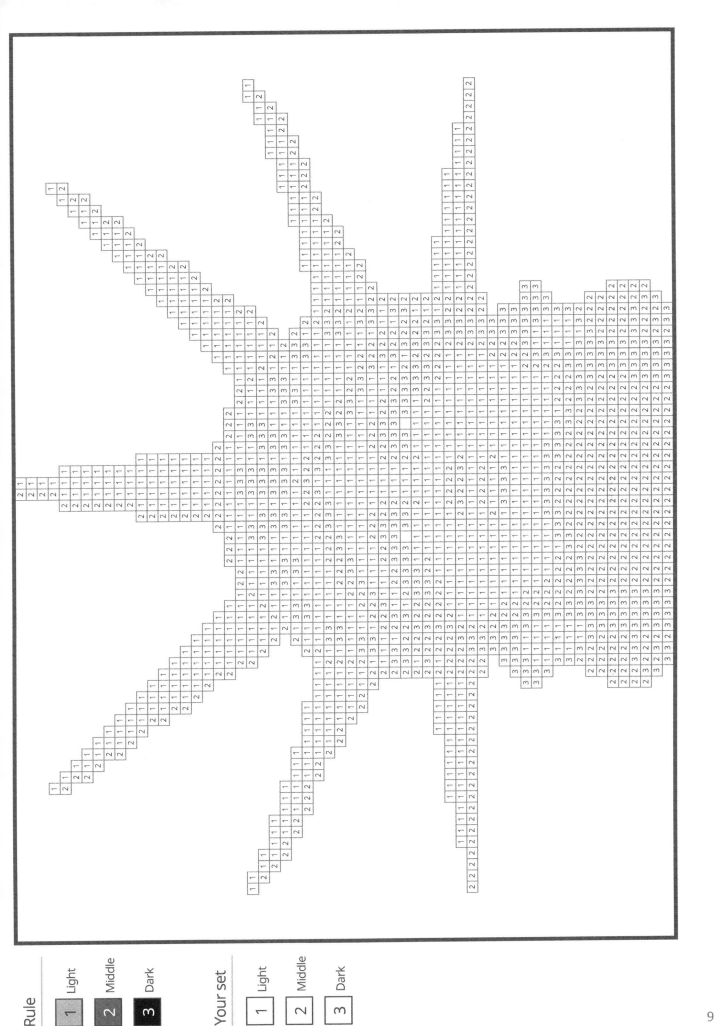

Rule

Light 1

Middle 2

Dark 3

Your set

1 Light

2 Middle

3 Dark

The Eiffel Tower

Rule

1 Light	2 Middle	3 Dark

Your set

1 Light	2 Middle	3 Dark

Mo'ai

Rule

| 1 | Light | 2 | Middle | 3 | Dark |

Your set

| 1 | Light | 2 | Middle | 3 | Dark |

The Tower of Pisa

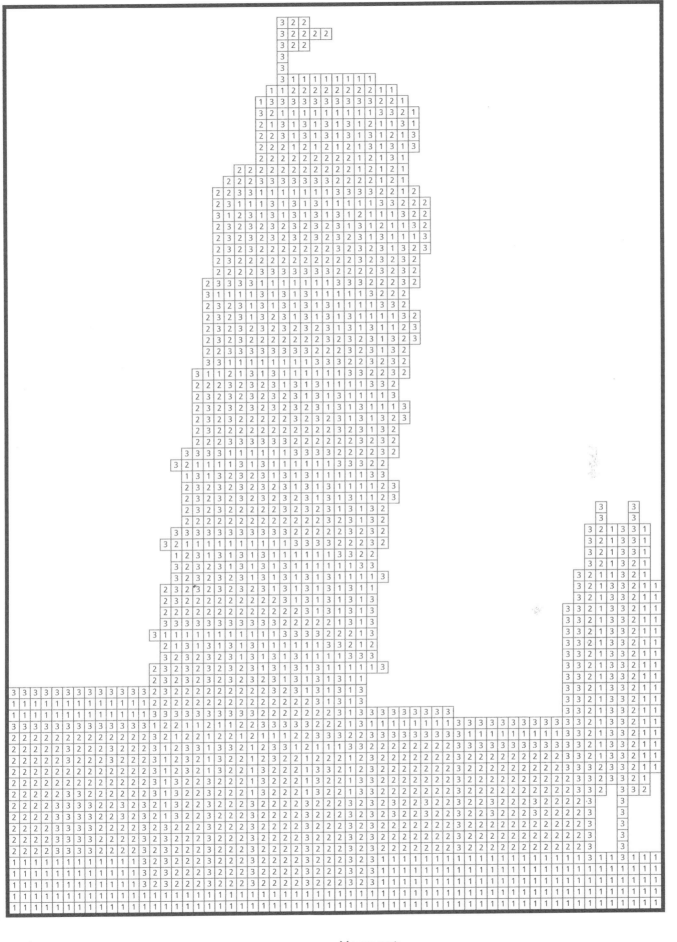

Rule

Your set

| 1 | Light | 2 | Middle | 3 | Dark |

15

The Statue
of the Bear and
the Strawberry
Tree

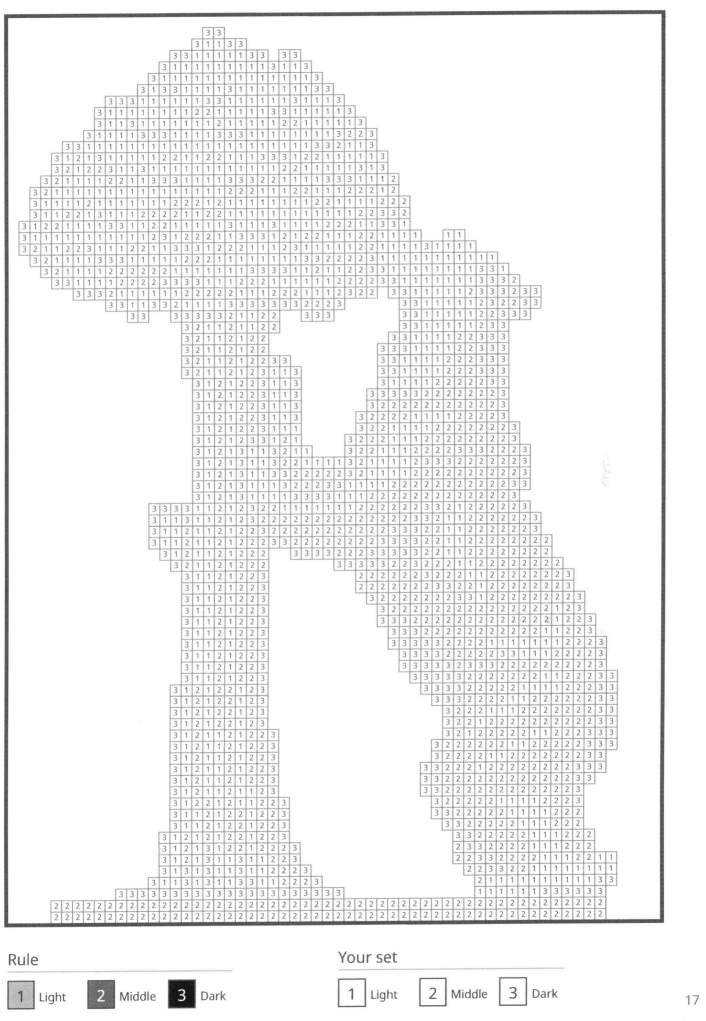

Rule

| 1 | Light | 2 | Middle | 3 | Dark |

Your set

| 1 | Light | 2 | Middle | 3 | Dark |

The Burj Al Arab

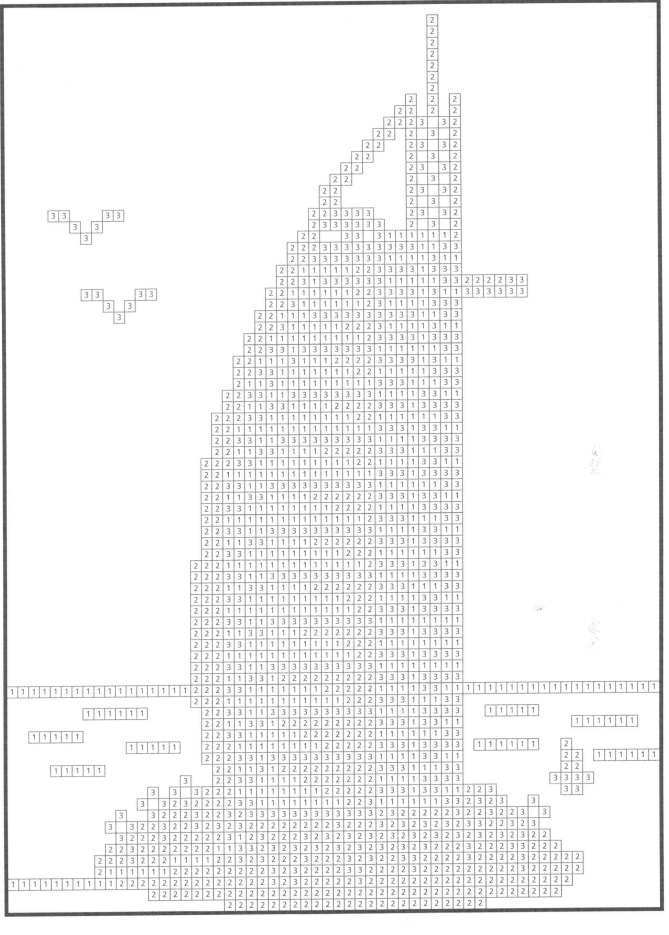

Rule

1 Light	2 Middle	3 Dark

Your set

1 Light	2 Middle	3 Dark

The Motherland Calls

Rule

1 Light 2 Middle 3 Dark

Your set

1 Light 2 Middle 3 Dark

Notre-Dame de Paris

Rule

| 1 | Light | 2 | Middle | 3 | Dark |

Your set

| 1 | Light | 2 | Middle | 3 | Dark |

23

The Little Mermaid

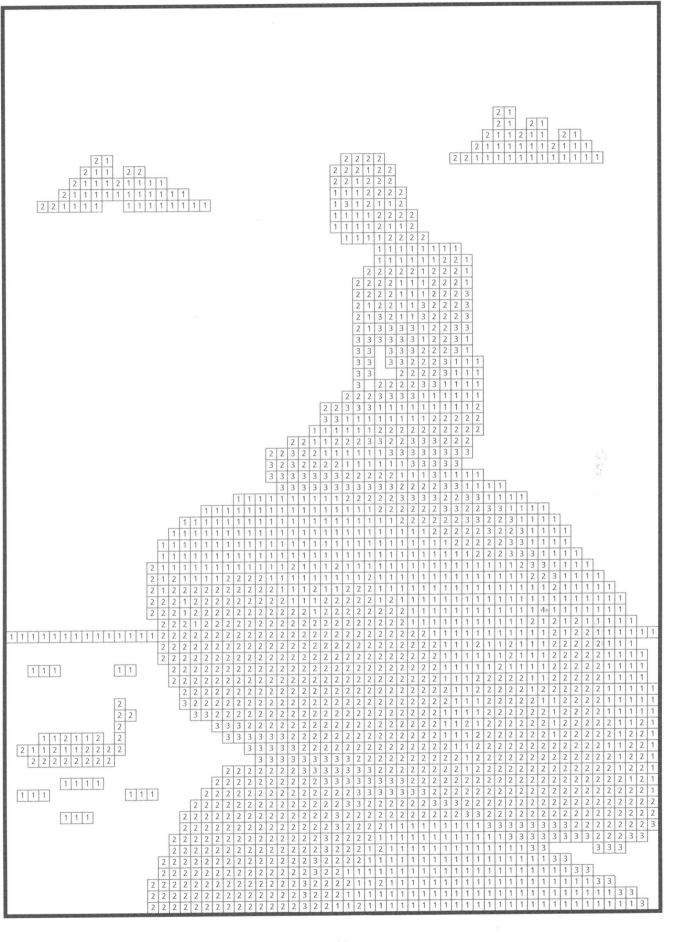

Rule

1 Light	**2** Middle	**3** Dark

Your set

1 Light	2 Middle	3 Dark

Petra

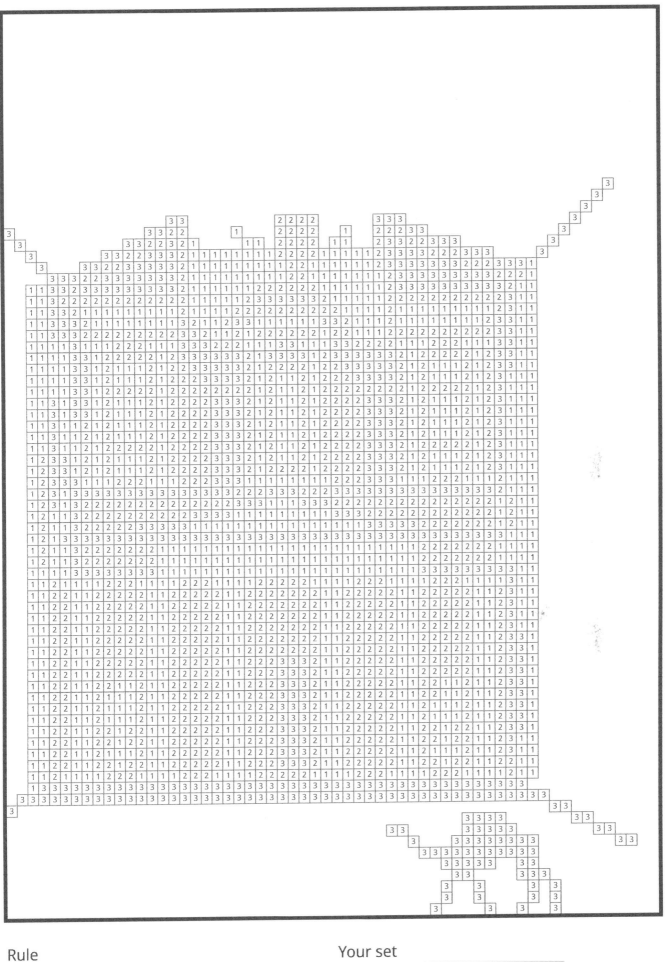

Rule

| 1 | Light | 2 | Middle | 3 | Dark |

Your set

| 1 | Light | 2 | Middle | 3 | Dark |

The African Renaissance Monument

Rule

| 1 | Light | 2 | Middle | 3 | Dark |

Your set

| 1 | Light | 2 | Middle | 3 | Dark |

Mount Rushmore
National Memorial

Rule

Light 1

Middle 2

Dark 3

Your set

1 Light

2 Middle

3 Dark

Tower Bridge

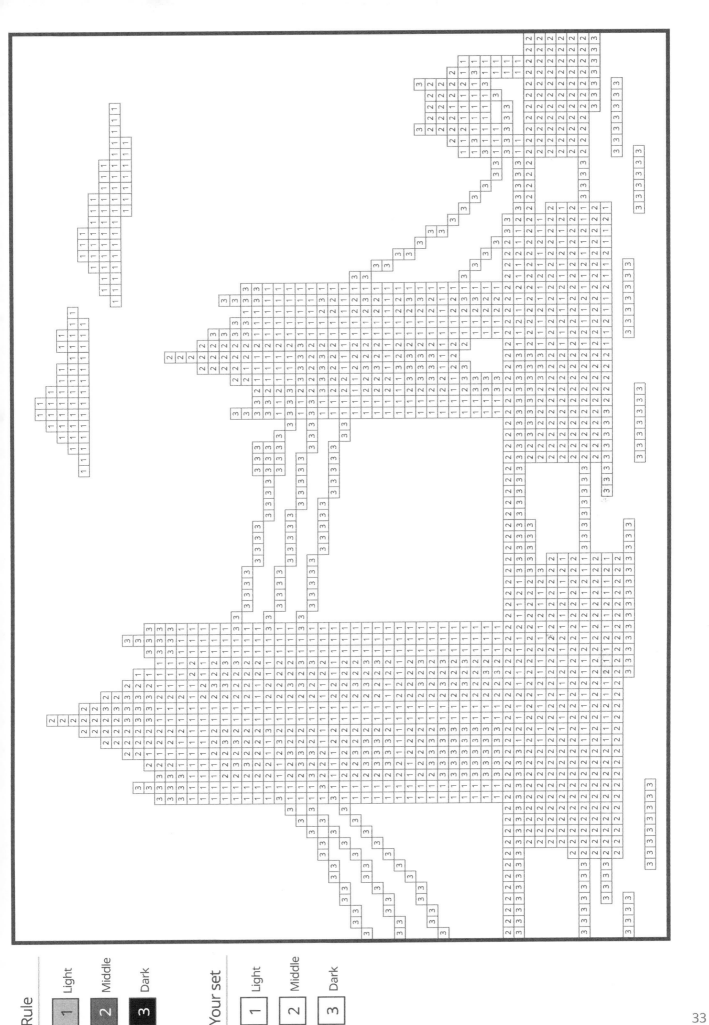

Rule

1	Light
2	Middle
3	Dark

Your set

1	Light
2	Middle
3	Dark

The Taj Mahal

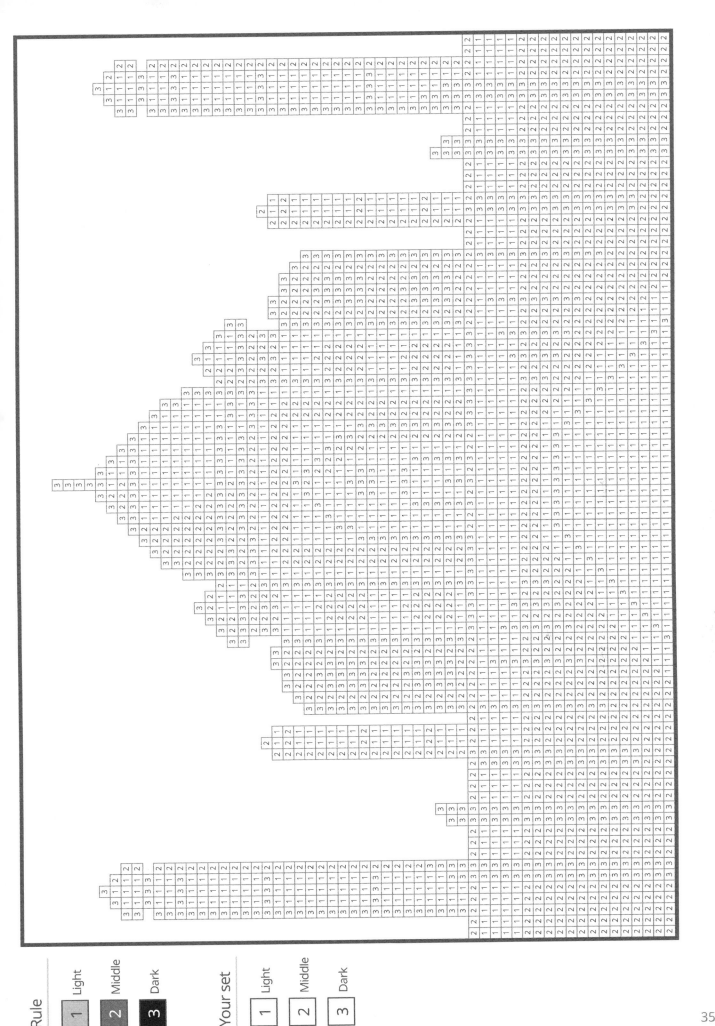

Rule

Light ▢ 1

Middle ▢ 2

Dark ▢ 3

Your set

Light ▢ 1

Middle ▢ 2

Dark ▢ 3

The Giza Pyramid Complex & The Great Sphinx of Giza

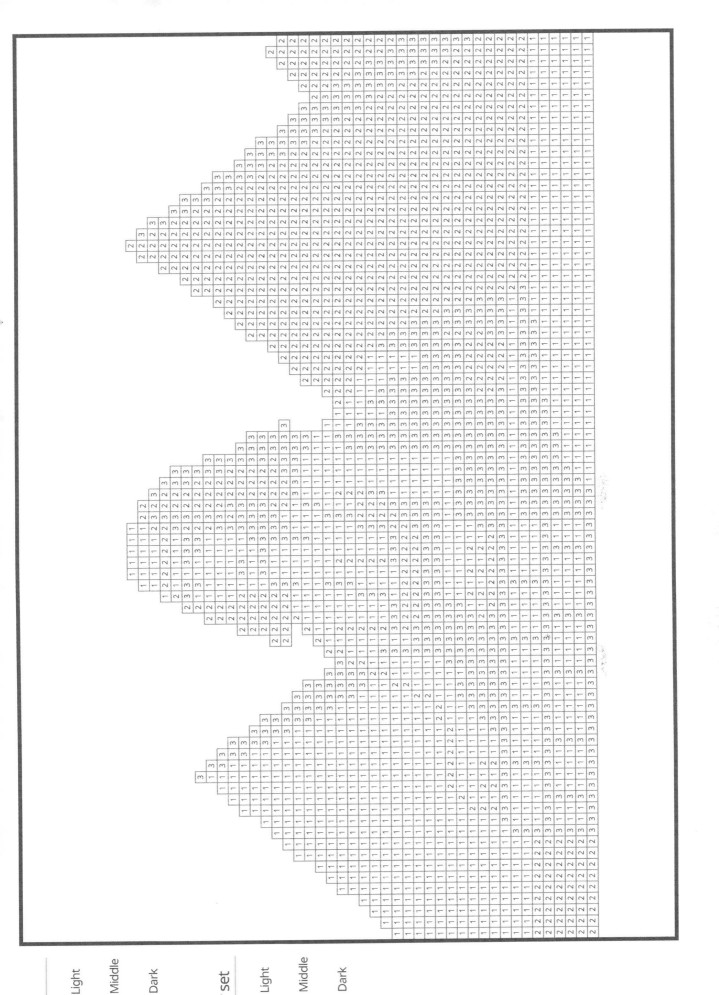

Rule

Light
1

Middle
2

Dark
3

Your set

Light
1

Middle
2

Dark
3

The Colosseum

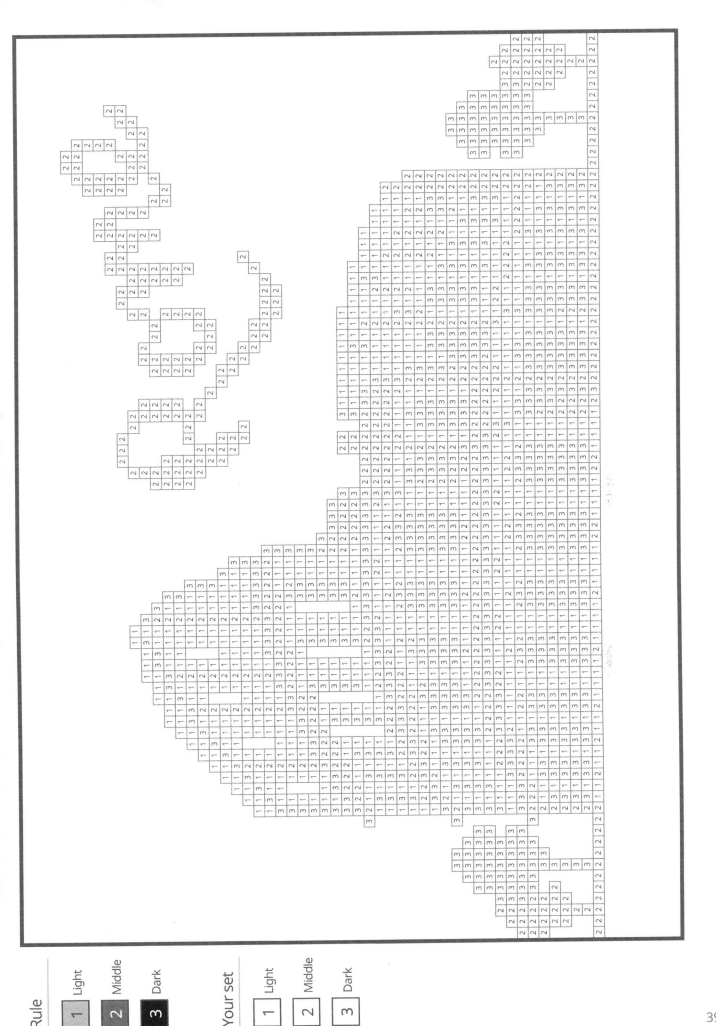

Rule

Light 1

Middle 2

Dark 3

Your set

Light 1

Middle 2

Dark 3

Machu Picchu

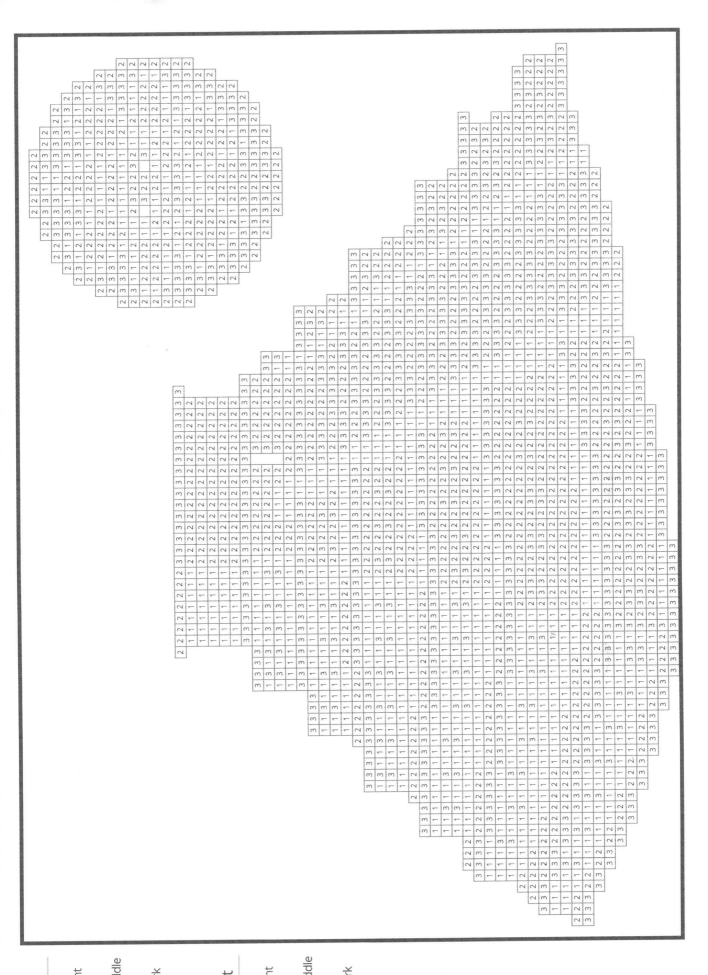

Rule

Light 1
Middle 2
Dark   3

Your set

Light 1
Middle 2
Dark   3

The Trojan Horse

Rule

Light 1

Middle 2

Dark 3

Your set

1 Light

2 Middle

3 Dark

The Temple
of Heaven

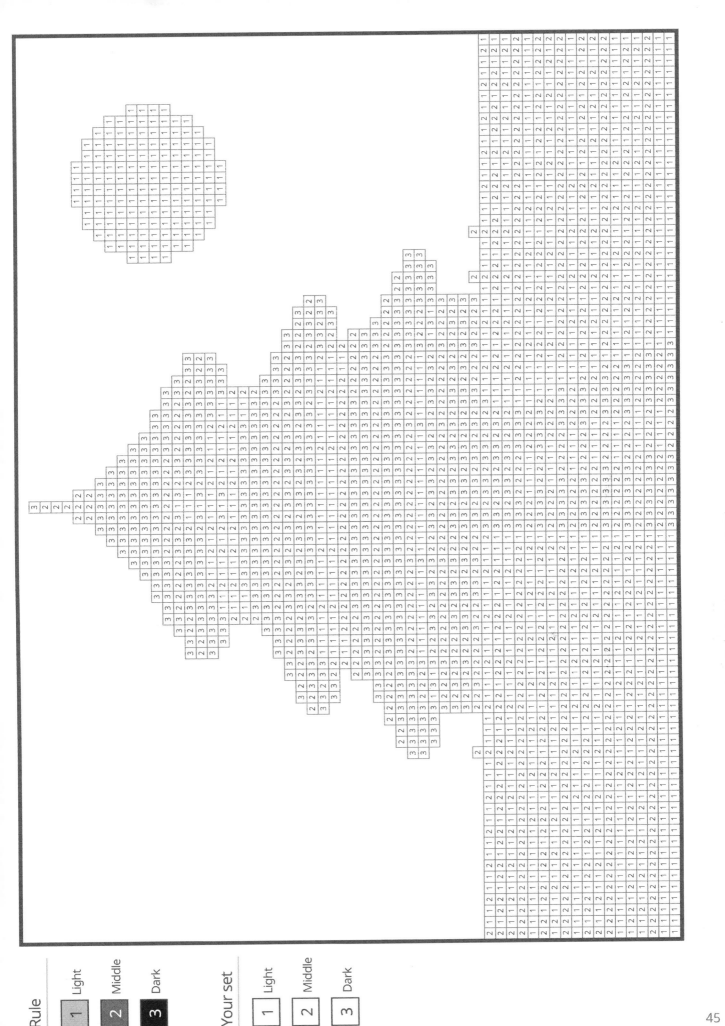

45

The Sydney Opera House

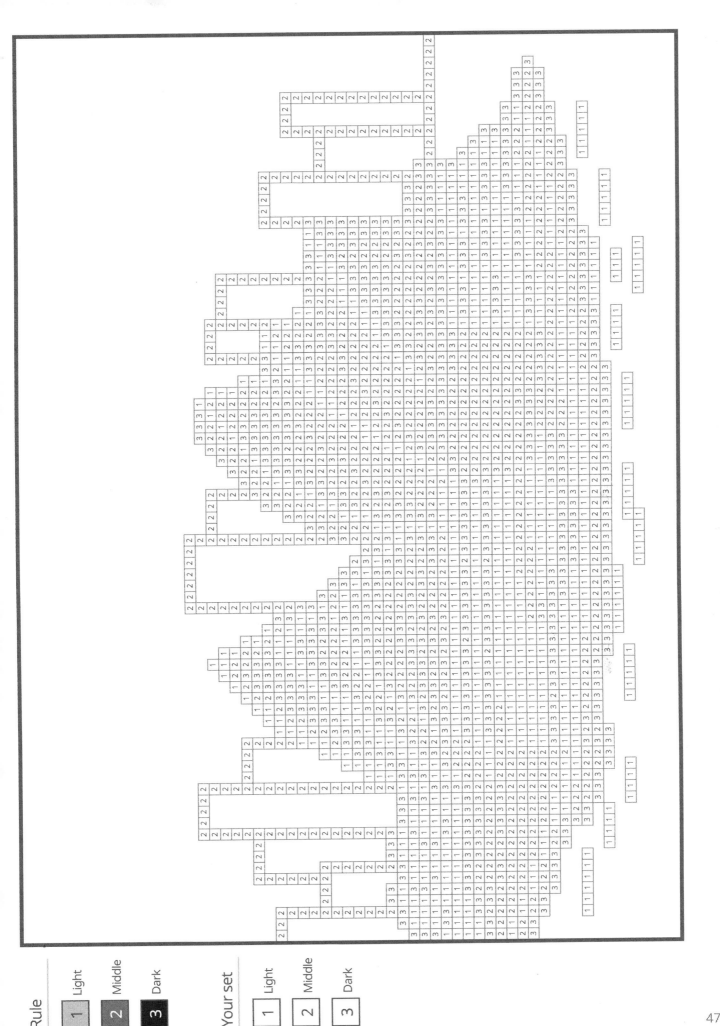

Rule

1 Light
2 Middle
3 Dark

Your set

1 Light
2 Middle
3 Dark

47

Gal Vihara
(The Stone Shrine)

Rule

1 Light

2 Middle

3 Dark

Your set

1 Light

2 Middle

3 Dark

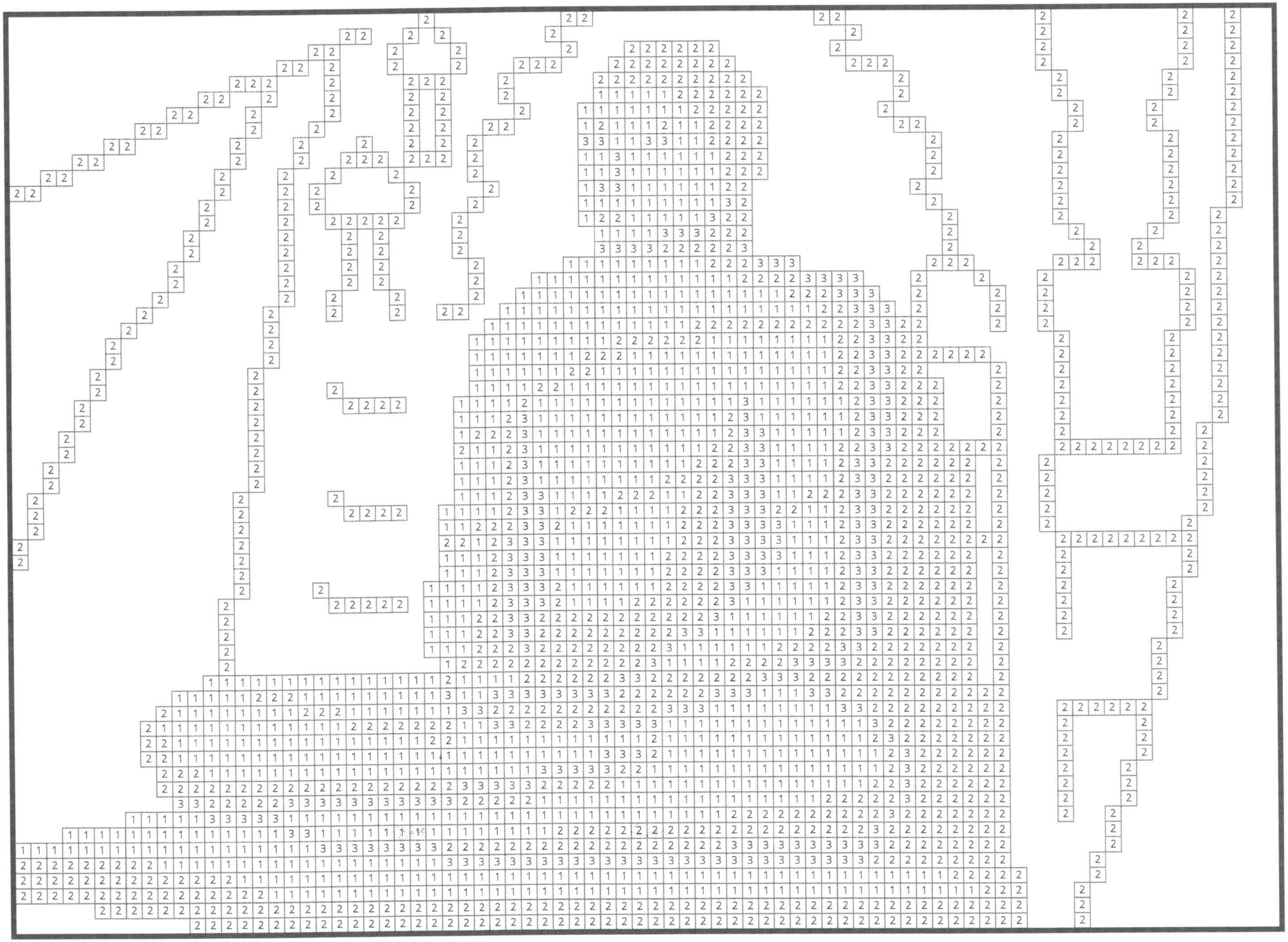

Aurora, the Protected cruiser

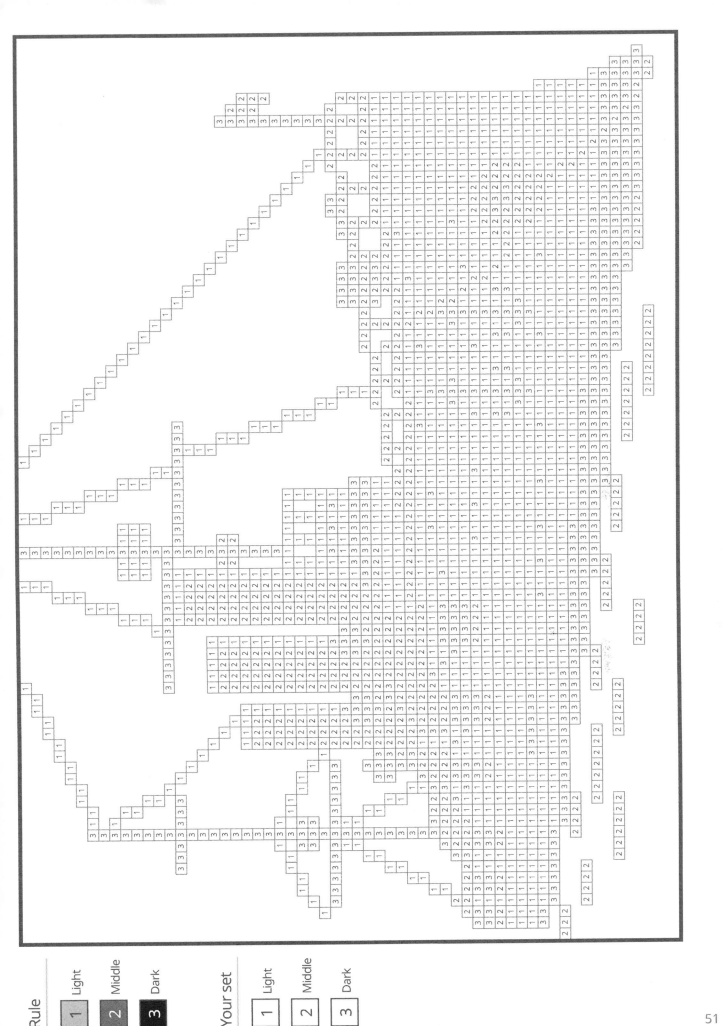

Rule

1	Light
2	Middle
3	Dark

Your set

1	Light
2	Middle
3	Dark

Christ the Redeemer

Rule

1 Light
2 Middle
3 Dark

Your set

1 Light
2 Middle
3 Dark

Guanyin statue
with 8 hands

Rule

Light
1

Middle
2

Dark
3

Your set

Light
1

Middle
2

Dark
3

The Great Wall
of China

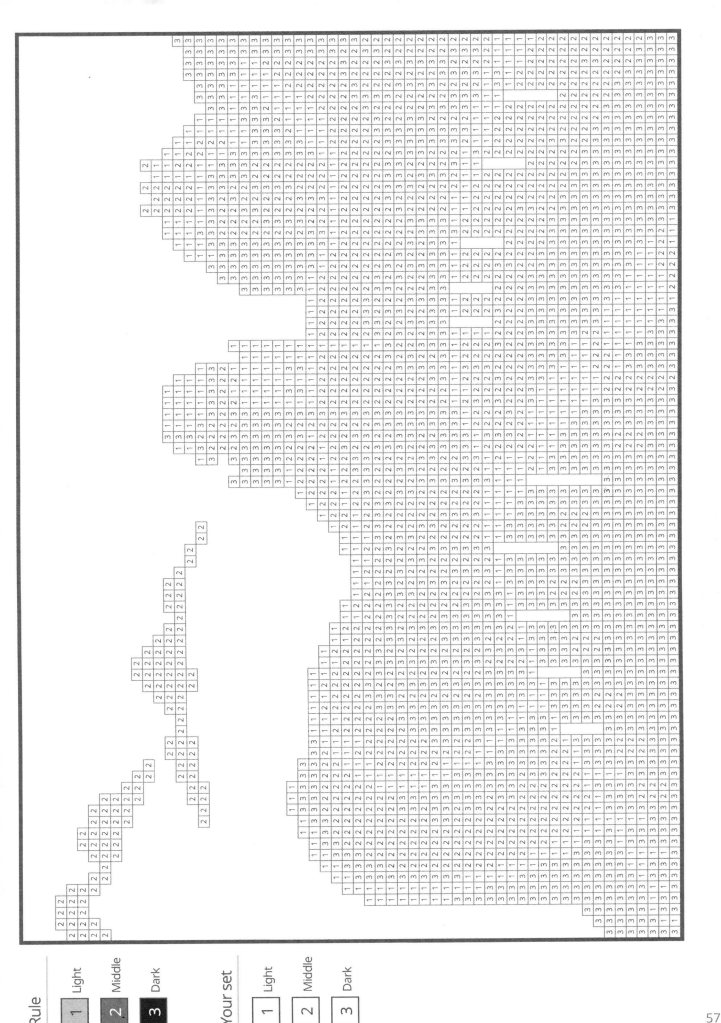

Rule

Light 1

Middle 2

Dark 3

Your set

Light 1

Middle 2

Dark 3

WE ARE THE BELBA FAMILY.

Thank you for your choice.

All books are made with love for People and Nature.

We appreciate your feedback with a small review of the book on Amazon, Facebook, or Instagram.

If you tag your colored pages as #belbafamily, we share your work on our social media pages.

You help us to make our books better.

Stay safe and happy coloring!

Follow us:

[f] https://www.facebook.com/belbafamily/

[o] Belba Family

[t] @BelbaFamily

You and your artworks inspired us to open the Belba Family Shop, where you can find different merch with best designs from our books!

[o] Belba Family Shop

[cart] BELBA.redbubble.com

TRY THE OTHER BOOK SERIES BY THE BELBA FAMILY:

The MOSAIC color by number ART activity book series includes:

- TRAVEL MOSAIC. Color by Number ART activity book.
- ANIMAL MOSAIC. Color by number ART activity book.

Color by number & coloring version books:

- CHRISTMAS & TRAVEL MOSAICS. An adult book with relaxing pages of Christmas scenes around the world.
- THE MONEY BOOK. An adult magic book with Money & Richness symbols to color.
- FAIRIES AROUND US. Stained Glass & Magic Mosaics. An adult Book for relaxation and stress relief.

PUZZLE COLOR BY NUMBER CLEVER BOOK SERIES:

BEGINNER level
(no background):

- SIMPLE BEAUTY
- HUMAN FACES

ADVANCED level
(with background):

- EXOTIC LIFE
- SECRET PATTERNS

STONE MOSAIC SERIES:

- BOOK 1
- BOOK 2
- BOOK 3

3 COLORS SERIES:

- CELEBRITIES
- ANIMALS & BIRDS
- TRAVEL

MYSTERY MOSAICS books series with 3*3 mm. sections:

- MYSTERY MOSAICS. PASSION
- MYSTERY MOSAICS. DOGS
- MYSTERY MOSAICS. WOMAN
- SQUARE MANDALAS (Book 1)
- MYSTERY MOSAICS. GALLERY
- MYSTERY MOSAICS. WOW, CATS!
- SQUARE MANDALAS. ANIMALS IN PATTERNS (Book 2)
- MYSTERY MOSAICS. CINEMA
- LISA'S GARDEN. SQUARE MANDALAS, PATTERNS, AND MORE
- MYSTERY MOSAICS. WOW, ANIMALS!
- MYSTERY MOSAICS. FLOWERS
- MYSTERY MOSAICS. ARIANE'S VINTAGE COLLECTION
- PARTY PATTERNS
- ALL ABOUT CHRISTMAS
- SQUARE MANDALAS (Book 3)
- MYSTERY MOSAICS. SECRET PATTERNS
- MYSTERY MOSAICS. WOW, AFRICA!

And more...

HAPPY COLORING!

Printed in Great Britain
by Amazon